Dick Whittington

Retold by Annette Smith
Illustrated by Elise Fowler

NELSON PRICE MILBURN

Once upon a time, in England, there was a boy called Dick Whittington. His parents had died when he was very young, and he was all alone in the world. He had no one to look after him, and he was often hungry.

Dick Whittington had heard about the great town of London, and he decided to go there to seek his fortune. One day, a large wagon drove through the village, so Dick asked the wagon driver if he could give him a ride. The driver, who was a kind man, agreed, and soon Dick was sitting in the wagon, on his way to London.

When the wagon arrived at the gates of London Town, Dick was very excited. He had never seen so many people. He walked up and down the busy streets asking for work. But no one was interested in a poor country boy, and everyone told him to go away.

At last, tired and exhausted from lack of food, Dick lay down in the doorway of a large house. In the morning, the cook opened the door and shouted at him to go away. But then Mr Fitzwarren, who was the master of the house, appeared. He was a very rich merchant.

"Why are you lying here, boy?" he asked kindly. "You look old enough to work. Why aren't you earning a living?"

"Please, sir," replied Dick, "I am faint with hunger. I would gladly work if I could find a job."

Mr Fitzwarren felt sorry for Dick, and he ordered the cook to give him a meal and find him some work in the kitchen.

The cook was annoyed about this, and she bullied Dick. No matter how hard he worked in the kitchen scrubbing the floor, washing the pots, and chopping wood for the fire, she shouted at him and often beat him. He had to sleep up in the attic with the mice and the rats.

Mr Fitzwarren had a daughter, Miss Alice, who was as kind as her father. She felt sorry for Dick, and she told the bad-tempered cook to treat him more kindly.

One day, Dick earned a penny for cleaning shoes. The next day, he saw a cat for sale in the market place. He bought it with his penny, which was all the money he had in the world. Then Dick took the cat to the attic, and at last he was no longer bothered by the rats and the mice. The cat was an excellent mouser.

Not long after that, one of Mr Fitzwarren's ships was ready to sail to Africa with a cargo of goods to trade. The kind merchant always invited his servants to send something for sale on every ship, so that they had a chance to make their fortunes, too.

When it was Dick's turn, he had nothing to offer.

Miss Alice wanted to give Dick something but her father said, "No, it must be something that belongs to Dick himself."

"All that I own is my cat," said Dick.

"The cat will do," said Mr Fitzwarren.

Dick felt sad to see his cat go on board the ship. He missed his pet, as he had grown very fond of her. The cook went on scolding Dick every day, and now she made fun of him for sending a cat to make his fortune!

Soon the rats and mice came back to the attic, and Dick could not sleep at night. He became more unhappy than ever. He was so miserable that he decided to run away.

Dick crept out of the house the next morning, while it was dark, and walked north as far as Highgate.

He was sitting down to rest on a milestone when the church bells began to ring. As he listened they seemed to say...

Turn again, Whittington,
Turn again, Whittington,
Lord Mayor of London.

"Lord Mayor of London!" said Dick. The bells rang on.

Turn again, Whittington,
Turn again, Whittington,
Lord Mayor of London.

"If I am to be the Lord Mayor," thought Dick, "then I should stay in London. Perhaps if I try, I can put up with the bad-tempered cook, and the rats."

Dick made his way back to the house as quickly as he could, and slipped back inside before anyone noticed that he had left.

London
3 Miles

In the meantime, Mr Fitzwarren's ship had arrived at a port in an African kingdom. The king was keen to trade with the ship's captain, and invited him to his palace where a great feast was prepared. However, the captain was dismayed to see hundreds of rats and mice swarming over the food.

The king told the captain that he would give half his fortune to anyone who could get rid of the rats and mice that plagued his country. The captain thought of Dick's cat, back on board the ship.

The captain told the king that he had an animal called a cat that was very clever at catching rats and mice.

"A cat!" said the king. "What is a cat?"

"I want to see this animal," said the queen.

While the captain went back to the ship to get the cat, the king ordered his servants to prepare a second feast. But as soon as the food was laid out, the rats and the mice swarmed all over that, too.

When the captain arrived with Dick's cat, she jumped out of his arms and sprang on the rats and mice. Swiftly, the cat killed dozens of them.

The king and the queen were overjoyed. They gave the captain a casket of gold and jewels, not only for the cat, but also for her kittens that had been born during the journey.

The captain was very pleased when the king bought everything else the ship was carrying. With fresh food and water aboard, the captain set sail for England once more.

After a long journey, the ship arrived safely back in London Town. The captain told Mr Fitzwarren the story, and handed him the gold and jewels that the king had exchanged for the cat.

At once Mr Fitzwarren sent for Dick, who was embarrassed because he was wet and dirty from scrubbing the kitchen floor. Mr Fitzwarren told Dick about the fortune his cat had earned for him.

"You are a very rich young man, now," said Mr Fitzwarren, as he gave Dick the gold and jewels.

Dick did not want to take all the treasure. He gave some of it to Mr Fitzwarren and Miss Alice, who had both been so kind to him, and some to the ship's captain and his sailors who had looked after his fortune so well. He even gave a jewel to the bad-tempered cook!

As the years went by, Dick and Miss Alice grew to love one another, and Mr Fitzwarren gladly arranged their marriage, which was a splendid affair.

They lived happily for many years. Dick became a rich and successful silk merchant. But he never forgot what it had been like to be poor, and he always gave much of his money away to those who needed it.

In the end, Dick Whittington became Lord Mayor of London, just as the bells had foretold.

A play

Dick Whittington

People in the play

Reader

Ship's captain

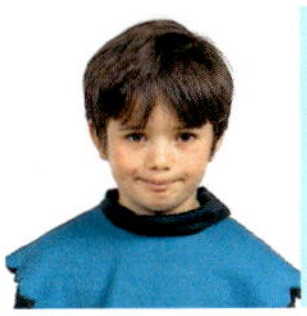

Dick Whittington

African king

Cat (mime only)

African queen

Miss Alice

Wagon driver

Mr Fitzwarren

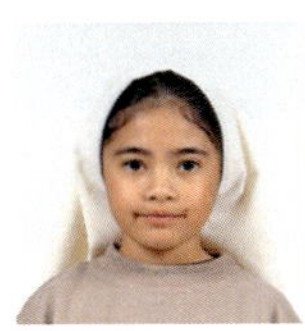

Cook

Bells

Scene One — In England

Reader

Once upon a time, in England, there was a boy called Dick Whittington. His parents had died when he was very young, and he was all alone in the world.

Dick Whittington

People have told me about the great town of London. I will go there to seek my fortune.

Reader

One day, a large wagon drove through the village. It was going to London.

Dick Whittington (to the wagon driver)

Please can I have a ride in your wagon?

Wagon driver

Climb up, boy, and I will take you there.

Reader

When the wagon arrived at the gates of London Town, Dick was very excited. He had never seen so many people. He walked up and down the busy streets, asking for work.

Dick Whittington

I am so tired and hungry. I cannot find anyone who will give me some work. I will have to shelter in this doorway tonight.

Reader

In the morning, the cook opened the door.

Cook

Go away, boy! Go away! You cannot sleep here!

Mr Fitzwarren

Cook! What is all this shouting about?

Cook

Master, this lazy boy has been sleeping here in the doorway. He will not go away.

Mr Fitzwarren (kindly)

Why are you lying here, boy? You look old enough to work. Why aren't you earning a living?

Dick Whittington

Please, sir, I am faint with hunger. I would gladly work if I could find a job.

Mr Fitzwarren

Cook, take this boy to the kitchen and give him a meal. Then find him some work to do.

Cook

Come with me, boy. I'll find you work to do, indeed I will. You can scrub the floors and wash the pots and chop wood for the fire.

Reader

No matter how hard Dick worked, the cook shouted at him and often beat him. He had to sleep in the attic with the mice and the rats. But Mr Fitzwarren had a daughter, Miss Alice, who was kind. She felt sorry for Dick.

Miss Alice

Cook, please do not bully this boy. Treat him more kindly.

Reader

One day, Dick earned a penny for cleaning shoes.

Dick Whittington

This is all the money that I have in the world. I need a cat to get rid of all the rats and the mice in the attic.

Reader

Dick bought a cat from the market. It was an excellent mouser, and soon Dick was no longer bothered by the rats and the mice. Not long after that, one of Mr Fitzwarren's ships was ready to sail to Africa. He gathered all of his servants before him.

Mr Fitzwarren

My ship will be leaving for Africa on the next tide. Each one of you can send something for sale with my cargo on the ship. You have a chance to make your fortunes, too.

Reader

When it was Dick's turn, he stood in front of Mr Fitzwarren looking unhappy.

Dick Whittington

Please, sir, I have nothing to give you.

Miss Alice

You can send something of mine, Dick.

Mr Fitzwarren

No, Alice. It must be something that belongs to Dick himself.

Dick Whittington

Please, sir, all that I own is my cat.

Mr Fitzwarren The cat will do.

Reader

Dick felt sad to see his cat go on board the ship. He missed his pet, as he had grown very fond of her. The cook went on scolding Dick every day, and now she made fun of him for sending a cat to make his fortune.

Dick Whittington

I cannot sleep at night. I miss my cat. The rats and mice have come back, now that she is not here. I am so unhappy. I will run away from this house forever.

Reader

Dick crept out of the house the next morning, while it was dark, and walked north as far as Highgate. He was sitting down on a milestone when the church bells began to ring.

Dick Whittington

The bells seem to be saying my name.

Bells (with singing voices)

Turn a-gain, Whit - tington,
Turn a-gain, Whit - tington,
Lord Mayor of London.

Dick Whittington

Lord Mayor of London! If I am to be the Lord Mayor, then I should stay in London. Perhaps if I try, I can put up with the bad-tempered cook, and the rats.

Reader

Dick made his way back to the house as quickly as he could, and slipped inside before anyone noticed that he had left. In the meantime, Mr Fitzwarren's ship had arrived at a port in an African kingdom. The king was keen to trade with the ship's captain.

Scene Two — In Africa

African king

Captain, I wish to talk business with you. Come to my palace this evening. I will put on a great feast in your honour.

Reader

When the captain sat down, he was dismayed to see rats and mice swarming over the food.

Ship's captain

Sir, why do you let rats and mice eat your food? Why don't you get rid of them?

African king

If only I could! These pests plague the whole country. I would give half my fortune to anyone who could get rid of them.

Ship's captain

On my ship, I have an animal called a cat. It is very clever at catching rats and mice.

African king

What is a cat? I have never heard of a cat!

African queen

I want to see this animal. Please go back to your ship and bring this cat creature to us.

African king

While you are away, I will have my servants prepare another feast.

Reader

But as soon as the food for the second feast was laid out, the rats and mice swarmed all over that, too. When the captain arrived with Dick's cat, she jumped out of his arms and sprang on the rats and mice.

African queen

Just look at that animal! It has killed dozens of rats and mice.

Ship's captain

I have more cats on board the ship. During our journey here, the cat had kittens.

African queen

We want these cats. We will give you a casket of gold and jewels for the cat and her kittens.

African king

I will buy all the cargo that you have, and I will stock your ship with fresh food and water.

Reader

The captain set sail for England once more. After a long journey, the ship arrived safely back in London Town. The captain told Mr Fitzwarren the whole story.

Scene Three — In England

Ship's captain (to Mr Fitzwarren)

Here are the jewels and gold that the African king gave me in exchange for Dick's cat.

Mr Fitzwarren (to the cook)

Tell Dick to come here to me at once.

Reader

Dick had been scrubbing the kitchen floor and he was wet and dirty. He felt embarrassed as he stood in front of Mr Fitzwarren.

Mr Fitzwarren

You are a very rich young man now, Dick. Here is the casket of gold and jewels that was exchanged for your cat. It is worth a fortune.

Dick Whittington

Oh, thank you, sir. But you must have some of the gold, and, Miss Alice, here are some jewels. Captain, here's some gold for you and your sailors. You all took care of my fortune so well. Cook, this jewel is for you.

Reader

Several years later, Dick became a rich silk merchant, and he married Miss Alice. They were always good to the poor. In the end, Dick Whittington became Lord Mayor of London, just as the bells had foretold.